BEAUTIFUL ANIMALS
Coloring Book

BEAUTIFUL ANIMALS
Coloring Book

SIRIUS

This edition published in 2024 by Sirius Publishing, a division of
Arcturus Publishing Limited,
26/27 Bickels Yard, 151–153 Bermondsey Street,
London SE1 3HA

ISBN: 978-1-3988-4476-6
CH011805NT

Printed in China

Introduction

The natural world is a favorite subject for coloring and this collection of artworks brings together 45 delightful images of animals of all kinds. All have been chosen as particularly attractive examples of the creatures they depict. Some are true to life, while others have been embellished with flowers or other patterns. You'll find alluring antelopes and gorgeous gibbons, exquisite elephants and beauteous bears, along with magnificent mice and ravishing raccoons.

All you need is your imagination, somewhere to spread out this book, and a plentiful selection of coloring pens or pencils. You can go true to life with the color or create your own schemes. Just choose an image and create your own beautiful animal portrait.

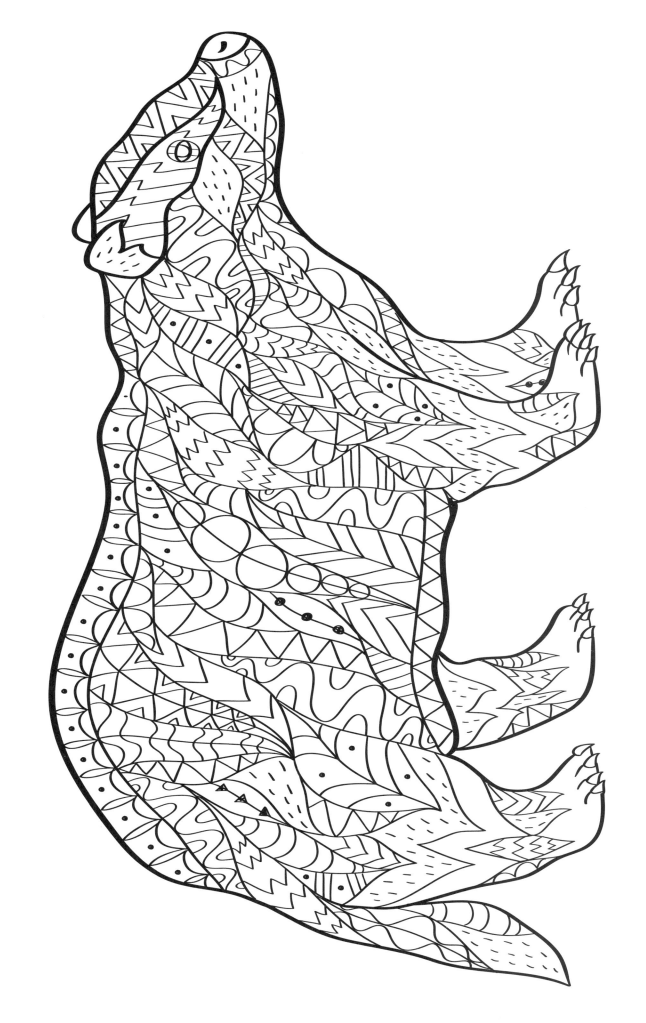

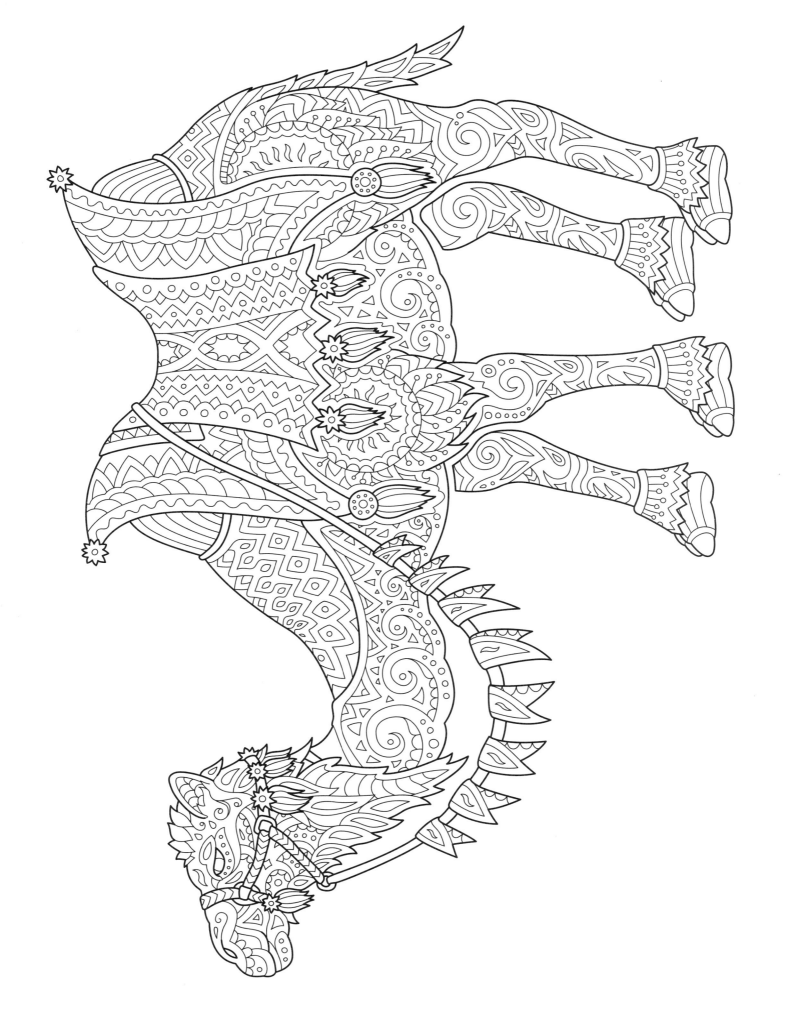

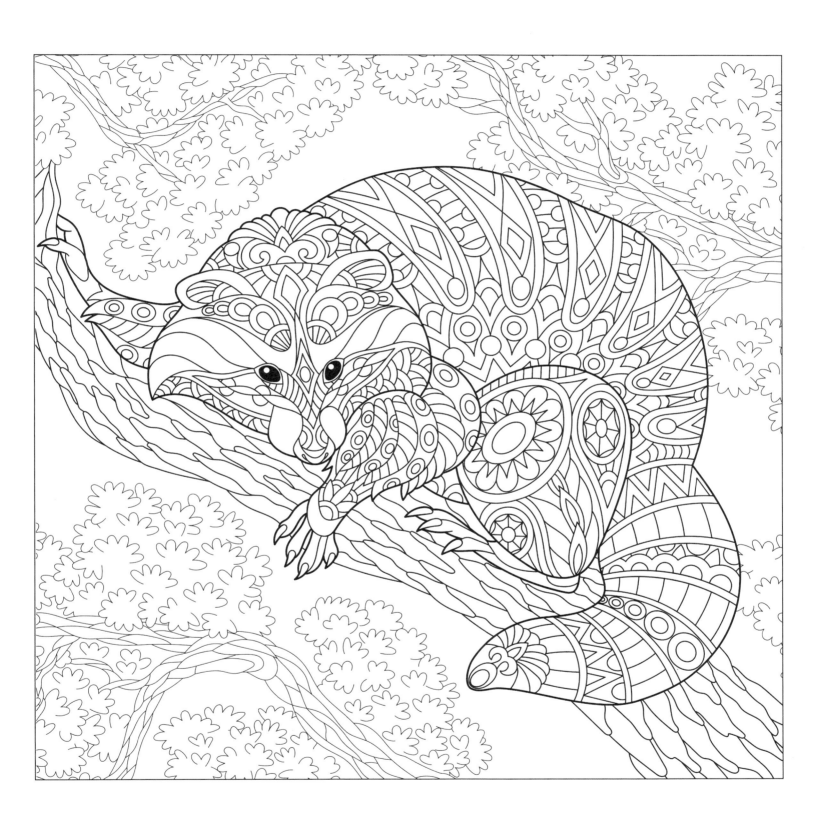

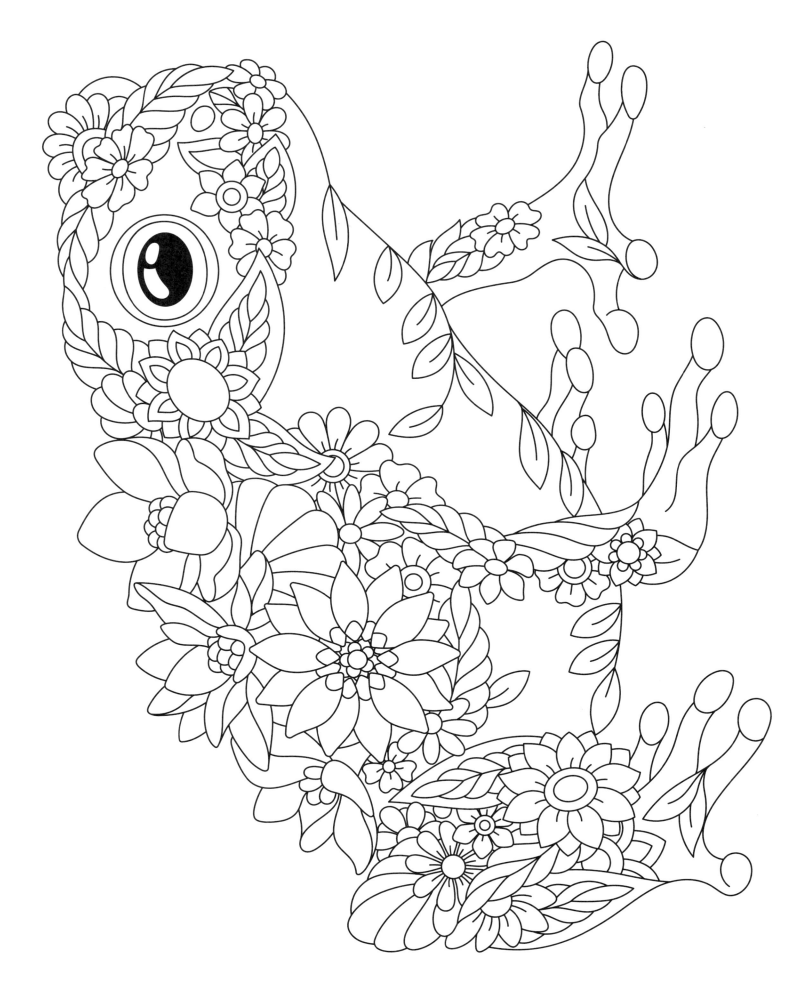

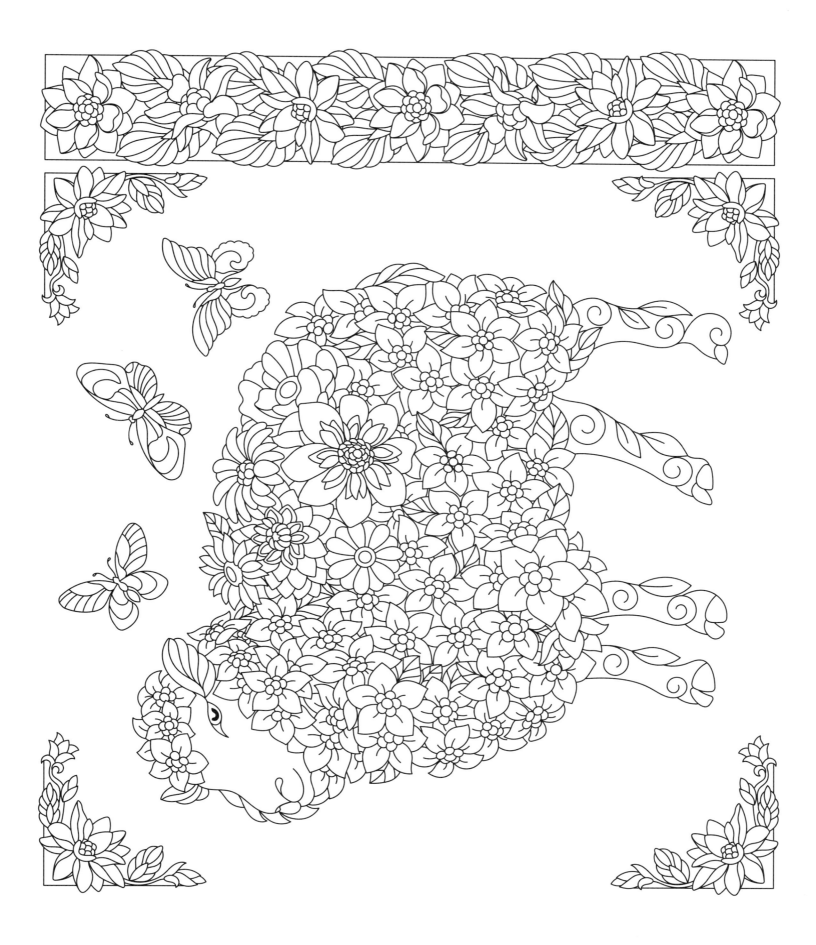

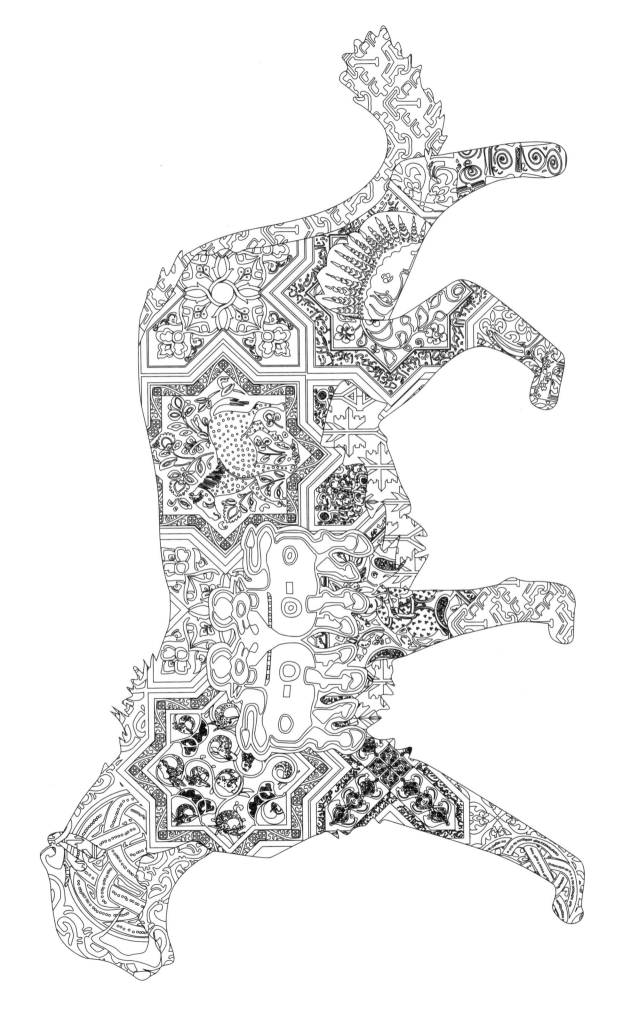